A Guide for Using

The Hobbit

in the Classroom

Based on the novel written by J.R.R. Tolkien

*This guide written by **John and Patty Carratello***

Illustrated by Sue Fullam

The authors wish to thank Syndi Hillis for her valuable help.

Teacher Created Resources, Inc.
6421 Industry Way
Westminster, CA 92683
www.teachercreated.com
ISBN: 978-1-55734-405-2
©1992 Teacher Created Resources, Inc.
Reprinted, 2012
Made in U.S.A.

Table of Contents

Introduction

A good book can touch our lives like a good friend. Within its pages are words and characters that can inspire us to achieve our highest ideals. We can turn to it for companionship, recreation, comfort, and guidance. It also gives us a cherished story to hold in our hearts forever.

In Literature Units, great care has been taken to select books that are sure to become good friends!

Teachers who use this literature unit will find the following features to supplement their own valuable ideas.

- Sample Lesson Plans
- Pre-reading Activities
- A Biographical Sketch and Picture of the Author
- A Book Summary
- Vocabulary Lists and Suggested Vocabulary Activities
- Chapters grouped for study, with each section including:
    - *quizzes*
    - *hands-on projects*
    - *cooperative learning activities*
    - *cross-curriculum connections*
    - *extensions into the reader's own life*
- Post-reading Activities
- Book Report Ideas
- Research Ideas and/or Literary Terms Activities
- A Culminating Activity
- Three Different Options for Unit Tests
- Bibliography
- Answer Key

We are confident that this unit will be a valuable addition to your planning, and hope that as you use our ideas, your students will increase the circle of "friends" that they can have in books!

Sample Lesson Plan

Each of the lessons suggested below can take from one to several days to complete.

LESSON 1

- Introduce and complete some or all of the pre-reading activities found on page 5.
- Read "About the Author" with your students. (page 6)
- Read the book summary with your students. (page 7)
- Introduce the vocabulary list for Section 1. (page 8) Ask students to find definitions.

LESSON 2

- Read Chapters 1 through 3. As you read, place the vocabulary words in the context of the story and discuss their meanings.
- Choose a vocabulary activity. (page 9)
- Create a character out of papier mache. (page 11)
- Plan a camp out. (page l2)
- Discuss the book in terms of physical education. (page 13)
- Begin "Reading Response Journals." (page 14)
- Administer the Section 1 quiz. (page 10)
- Introduce the vocabulary list for Section 2. (page 8) Ask students to find definitions.

LESSON 3

- Read Chapters 4 through 7. Place the vocabulary words in context and discuss their meanings.
- Choose a vocabulary activity. (page 9)
- Learn about magic, and practice what you can! (page 16)
- Create riddles for each other to solve. (page 17)
- Discuss the book in terms of science. (page 18)
- Discuss and explain common proverbs. (page 19)
- Administer the Section 2 quiz. (page 15)
- Introduce the vocabulary list for Section 3. (page 8) Ask students to find definitions.

LESSON 4

- Read Chapters 8 through 11. Place the vocabulary words in context and discuss their meanings.
- Choose a vocabulary activity. (page 9)
- Learn about forests. (page 21)
- Dramatize the prejudging of others in original stories. (page 22)
- Discuss book in terms of social studies. (page 23)
- Discuss the changes that are brought about by challenges. (page 24)
- Administer the Section 3 quiz. (page 20)
- Introduce the vocabulary list for Section 4. (page 8) Ask students to find definitions.

LESSON 5

- Read Chapters 12 through 14. Place the vocabulary words in context and discuss their meanings.
- Choose a vocabulary activity. (page 9)
- Design armor. (page 26)
- Stage a talk show. (page 27)
- Discuss the book in terms of language arts. (page 28)
- Design family trees. (page 29)
- Administer the Section 4 quiz. (page 25)
- Introduce the vocabulary list for Section 5. (page 8) Ask students to find definitions.

LESSON 6

- Read Chapters 15 through 19. Place the vocabulary words in context and discuss their meanings.
- Choose a vocabulary activity. (page 9)
- Make something for the birds. (page 31)
- Design a "Middle Earth Gazette." (page 32)
- Discuss the book in terms of music. (page 33)
- Discuss the wisdom age has to offer. (page 34)
- Administer the Section 5 quiz. (page 30)

LESSON 7

- Discuss any questions your students may have about the story. (page 35)
- Assign book report and research projects. (pages 36 and 37)
- Begin work on a culminating activity. (pages 38, 39, 40, and 41)

LESSON 8

- Administer one, two, and/or three unit tests. (pages 42, 43, and 44)
- Discuss the test answers and possibilities.
- Discuss the students' enjoyment of the book.
- Provide a list of related reading for your students. (page 45)

Before the Book

Before you begin reading The Hobbit with your students, do some pre-reading activities to stimulate interest and enhance comprehension. Here are some activities that might work well in your class.

1. Predict what the story might be about just by hearing the title.

2. Predict what the story might be about just by looking at the cover illustration.

3. Discuss other books by J.R.R. Tolkien that students may have heard about or read.

4. Answer these questions:

   Are you interested in:

   - adventure stories set in a world of fantasy?

   - stories in which the main character must learn how to survive by using his/her own resourcefulness?

   - stories which involve special friendships between characters who seem to be "worlds" apart?

   - stories about those whose lifestyles are quite different from your own?

   Would you ever:

   - leave your comfortable home to embark upon an adventure?

   - fight against great odds to help others win back something that was rightfully theirs, but did not in any way belong to you?

   - stay overnight with strangers who were very peculiar?

   - have the courage to face a dragon, or something just as fearsome?

5. Create a fantasy world in which you would like to live for a time. Describe in detail.

6. Work in groups or as a class to create your own plot, setting, and characters for a fantasy story

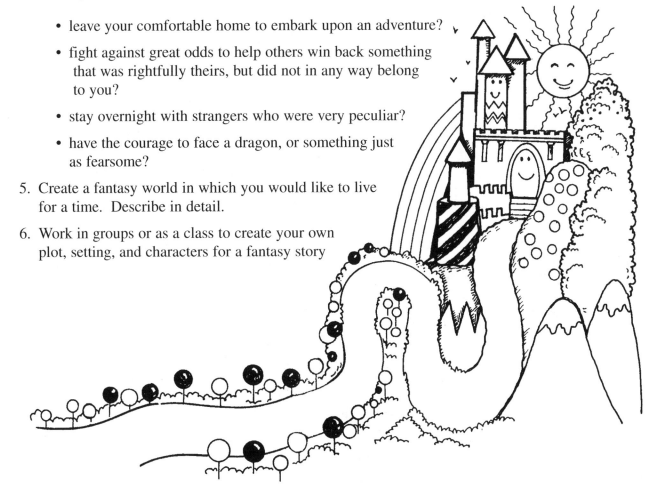

About the Author

J.(John) R.(Ronald) R.(Reuel) Tolkien (pronounced Tohl-keen) was born on January 3, 1892 in Bloemfontein, South Africa. As a baby, he was once kidnapped by the family servant who wanted to show the young boy off to his native friends. Tolkien's early memories of South Africa included parched country, hot days, a snake bite, and a tarantula sting.

In 1895, Tolkien's mother Mabel returned to England with young Tolkien and his brother Hilary. After his father's death in 1896, the family stayed at a cottage in Sarehole Mill where the rest of his childhood was lived relatively carefree. His summers were filled with picking flowers, inventing ogres, adventuring, and creating stories. At seven he wrote his first story about a dragon. In school, Tolkien became fascinated with languages and began to invent his own. He also loved trees. He would sketch them, converse with them, and plan stories for them to live within.

After the death of his mother in 1904, Father Francis Morgan became his guardian. While living with him, Tolkien met and fell in love with Edith Bratt. He attended college at Oxford University, joined the Army in 1915, and finally married Edith in 1916. He and Edith had four children, three boys and a girl. During the early years of his marriage, he worked on the staff of the *Oxford English Dictionary* and taught at Oxford University. He became friends with C.S. Lewis and, along with a few other college professors, they shared their writings. One of those writings was *The Hobbit,* begun in 1930 and published in 1936.

Something that hobbit lovers might find interesting is that Tolkien described himself as a hobbit.

> *"I am in fact a hobbit in all but size. I like gardens, trees, and unmechanized farmlands, I smoke a pipe, and like good plain food (unrefrigerated), but detest French cooking; I like, and even dare to wear in these dull days, ornamental waistcoats. I am fond of mushrooms (out of a field); have a very simple sense of humour (which even my appreciative critics find tiresome); I go to bed late and get up late (when possible). I do not travel much."*

> — as quoted in *Tolkien: A Biography* by Humphrey Carpenter (Houghton, 1977)

The publishers of The Hobbit encouraged Tolkien to write a sequel and he began to create *The Lord of the Rings* in 1936. He published *Volume I: The Fellowship of the Ring* and *Volume II: The Two Towers* in 1954. In 1955, the final book in the trilogy was published, *Volume III: The Return of the King.*

In 1959, Tolkien retired from his teaching job at Oxford and continued to write, publishing such works as *The Adventures of Tom Bombadil* in 1962 and *Smith of Wootton Major* in 1967. He loved writing and needed to write. He once said of himself that a pen was to him as a beak was to a hen!

On September 2, 1973, a perforated ulcer claimed Tolkien's life. His son Christopher edited some of his father's unpublished writings, and because of this we are able to enjoy other works Tolkien had created, such as *The Silmarillion.* Tolkien leaves behind a legacy which will be long remembered. He invites his readers to the fantastic world of Middle Earth, a world in which we can become immersed, fully believing that hobbits, dwarves, elves, and dragons just might be possible. He fills us with the magic of his dream.

The Hobbit

by J.R.R. Tolkien

Bilbo Baggins is a happy, sedentary sort of hobbit, leading a comfortable, predictable life filled with no wild adventures or daring risks—that is, until Gandalf comes to his door.

What Gandalf proposes to an overwhelmed Bilbo is the chance to be a burglar on a grand and dangerous adventure. His job would be to help the dwarves regain their lost fortune, a treasure that rests at the bottom of Lonely Mountain, guarded by the fierce dragon, Smaug. Reluctant, but curious, Bilbo accepts the position, a position that changes his life dramatically.

In the year-long journey that follows, Bilbo and his traveling companions encounter hazardous terrain and formidable foes. Many are the times Bilbo wishes to be in his warm, secure hobbit hole again. But the experience of adventure brings out the resourcefulness and courage in Bilbo's character, and these once latent strengths play an integral part in the dwarves' victorious recovery of their fortune.

The Hobbit invites readers to a fantasy world full of implausible, wonderful, memorable characters with whom we can often identify. Perhaps we, along with Bilbo Baggins, can learn to suspend what we are accustomed to doing and believing, and enter the captivating world of Middle Earth.

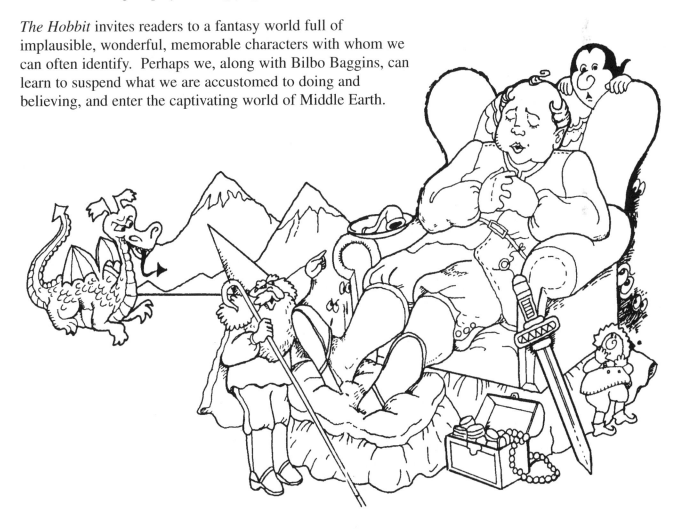

Vocabulary Lists

On this page are vocabulary lists which correspond to each sectional grouping of chapters. Vocabulary activity ideas can be found on page 9 of this book.

Section 1

audacious	morsel
cleave	mutton
conspirator	obstinately
defrayed	palpitating
depredations	paraphernalia
esteemed	parchment
estimable	plundering
flummoxed	requisite
flustered	scuttled
haughty	trifle
immense	venerable

Section 2

antiquity	groped
benighted	ingenious
boughs	marjoram
clamor	plight
commotion	throttled
deceptions	trestles
descendants	venture
droning	waistcoat
famished	yammering
gnarled	

Section 3

abominable	loathsome
accursed	ominous
bulbous	parchingly
cunning	plight
dreary	portcullis
flagon	promontory
frauds	ransom
gnawingly	suppressed
lichen	wary

Section 4

absurd	lair
aimlessly	perilous
benefactor	prophesying
brooded	radiance
creditable	reckoned
desolate	roused
drear	trill
dubious	valor
forges	vast
hoards	waning
inevitable	wily

Section 5

avenged	mustering
besiege	parley
caper	perils
carrion	precipice
commence	presumption
decrepit	prosperous
dominion	redeem
hauberk	siege
literally	wielded
mattocks	

8

Vocabulary Activity Ideas

You can help your students learn and retain the vocabulary in The Hobbit by providing them with interesting vocabulary activities. Here are a few ideas to try.

❑ People of all ages like to make and solve puzzles. Ask your students to make their own **Crossword Puzzles** or **Wordsearch Puzzles** using the vocabulary words from the story.

❑ Challenge your students to a **Vocabulary Bee**. This is similar to a spelling bee, but in addition to spelling each word correctly, the game participants must correctly define the words as well.

❑ Play **Vocabulary Concentration**. The goal of this game is to match vocabulary words with their definitions. Divide the class into groups of two to five students. Have students make two sets of cards the same size and color. On one set have them write the vocabulary words. On the second set have them write the definitions. All cards are mixed together and placed face down on a table. A player picks two cards. If the pair matches the words with its definition, the player keeps the cards and takes another turn. If the cards don't match, they are returned to their places face down, and another player takes a turn. Players must concentrate to remember the locations of words and their definitions. The game continues until all matches have been made.

❑ Have your students practice their writing skills by creating sentences and paragraphs in which multiple vocabulary words are used correctly. Ask them to share their **Compact Vocabulary** sentences and paragraphs with the class.

❑ Ask your students to create paragraphs which use the vocabulary words to present **Fantasy Lessons** that relate to the types of ideas and conflicts presented in the story.

❑ Challenge your students to use a specific vocabulary word from the story at least **Ten Times In One Day**. They must keep a record of when, how, and why the word was used.

❑ As a group activity, have students work together to create an **Illustrated Dictionary** of the vocabulary words.

❑ Play **Twenty Questions** with the entire class. In this game, one student selects a vocabulary word and gives clues about this word, one by one, until someone in the class can guess the word.

❑ Play **Vocabulary Charades**. In this game, vocabulary words are acted out.

You probably have many more ideas to add to this list. Try them. See if experiencing vocabulary on a personal level increases your students' vocabulary interest and retention!

Quiz

1. On the back of this paper, write a one paragraph summary of the major events in each chapter of this section. Then complete the rest of the questions on this page.

2. What is Gandalf's reputation?

   _____

   _____

3. According to the dwarves' song, where do they want to go, why do they wish to go there, and why did they leave in the first place? Answer on the back of this paper.

4. What is to be Bilbo's job on the adventure?

   _____

   _____

5. What is significant about the map Gandalf gives Thorin?

   _____

   _____

6. Describe what happens to Bilbo on his first attempt at "burglaring."

   _____

   _____

7. How does Gandalf trick the trolls? What then happens to them?

   _____

   _____

8. What are rune-letters? What are moon-letters? How are they significant?

   _____

   _____

9. What does Elrond tell the party about their swords?

   _____

   _____

10. On the back of this page, explain how you would have reacted if Gandalf and the dwarves had shown up at your house and invited you on their adventure.

Create a Character!

The Hobbit is full of unusual characters: dwarves, elves, dragons, trolls, and, of course, hobbits. Based on descriptions found in the book and by adding a touch of imagination, create a papier-mache replica of one of the characters you met in your reading of The Hobbit.

Making Papier-Mache Creatures

There are several ways to make papier-mache models. For this project, you will want to use the layering method.

- Tear newspaper into $\frac{1}{2}$ inch strips. Never use scissors to cut the paper, as it will leave a hard line at the edge. Be sure to tear all the strips you will need before beginning the project.

- Shape the outline of your model with balloons or wire.

- Dip the newspaper strips in the paste mixture (see recipe below) until all the paper is covered with paste.

- Layer the soaked strips on the model, building the shape with thicknesses of newspaper. You may need to tear strips into specific sizes to fit a corner or round an edge. Allow each layer to dry thoroughly before applying the next layer.

- As your model takes shape, you can add small balls of paste-soaked paper that you shape like clay to make noses, horns, and other "additions." Cover each addition with strips to make a permanent connection.

- Add a fine finish to your model by using colored or white tissue paper as the last layer.

- When thoroughly dry, models can be painted, beaded, ribboned, and dressed up in ways only your imagination can suggest!

Paste Mixture

Materials: mixing bowl
                          whisk or spoon
                          1 cup white flour
                          2 cups cold water
                          1 tablespoon salt

Directions: Mix together water, salt, and flour.
                          Stir well. Mixture can also be
                          heated until paste turns translucent.
                          Unused paste should be stored in the
                          refrigerator.

Camp Out

Bilbo wakes up the morning after the dwarves leave, believing they have left without him. When he discovers a message telling him to meet the dwarves at The Green Dragon Inn at 11:00 sharp, only ten minutes away, he runs "as fast as his furry feet could carry him down the lane . . . and found he had come without even a pocket handkerchief." The dwarves, however, have an extra cloak, and a pony "slung with all kinds of baggage, parcels, and paraphernalia."

Imagine you must pack for the same adventure the dwarves have planned. What would you take? Work in groups of three or four people to compile a list of necessities for your travel. Each group member must contribute at least three "essentials" for your group list. Remember, there are no modern conveniences, and you and a pony must be able to carry everything you plan to take. You will be gone for one month.

Continue to work in your group to answer these questions:

- If you had to cut your list in half, what would you keep? Put a star next to those items.
- Compare your list with other groups.
    - Do others have something important you forgot?
    - How are they similar?
    - How are they different?
- How would packing for a trip in your world be different from packing for a trip in the world of The Hobbit?

Physical Education: Sports History

Old Took, Bilbo's grandfather on his mother's side, had a great-granduncle who was long remembered.

> *". . .Bullroarer, who was so huge (for a hobbit) that he could ride a horse. He charged the ranks of the goblins of Mount Gram in the Battle of the Green Fields, and knocked their king Golfimbul's head clean off with a wooden club. It sailed a hundred yards through the air and went down a rabbit-hole, and in this way the battle was won and the game of Golf invented at the same moment."*

Choose a sport and create a brief history about a way in which it may have been "invented." Try to capsule the idea in a short paragraph, as Tolkien did. Your story may be realistic or fantasy! Write your finished sports history here. Cut out the story and display it on a bulletin board.

Reading Response Journals

One great way to insure that the reading of *The Hobbit* touches each student in a personal way is to include the use of Reading Response Journals in your plans. In these journals, students can be encouraged to respond to the story in a number of ways. Here are a few ideas.

- Ask students to create a journal for *The Hobbit*. Initially, just have them assemble lined and un-lined pages with a blank page for the journal's cover. As they read the story, they may draw a design on the cover that helps tell the story for them.

- Tell them that the purpose of the journal is to record their thoughts, ideas, observations, and questions as they read *The Hobbit*.

- Provide students with, or ask them to suggest, topics from the story that would stimulate writing. Here are a few examples from the chapters in Section 1.

    – When Gandalf came to Bilbo's hobbit hole, he presented Bilbo with an opportunity for adventure that both frightened and intrigued him. Describe a time you have been both frightened and intrigued by something you were asked to do.

    – The dwarves and Gandalf expected Bilbo Baggins to be able to do a job that he didn't think he could do. How would you feel if you were Bilbo Baggins?

- After the reading of each chapter, students can write one or more new things they learned in the chapter.

- Ask students to draw their responses to certain events or characters in the story, using the blank pages in their journals.

- Tell students that they may use their journals to record "diary-type" responses.

- Encourage students to bring their journal ideas to life! Ideas generated from their writing can be used to create plays, debates, stories, songs, and art displays.

- Allow students time to write in their journals daily.

Explain to the students that their Reading Response Journals can be evaluated in a number of ways. Here are a few ideas.

- Personal reflections will be read by the teacher, but no corrections or letter grades will be assigned. Credit is given for effort, and all students who sincerely try will be awarded credit. If a "grade" is desired for this type of entry, you could grade according to the number of journal entries for the number of journal assignments. For example, if five journal assignments were made and the student conscientiously completes all five, then he or she should receive an "A."

- Nonjudgmental teacher responses should be made as you read the journals to let the students know that you are reading and enjoying their journals.

- If you would like to grade something for form and content, ask the students to select one of their entries and "polish it" according to the writing process.

Quiz

1. On the back of this paper, write a one paragraph summary of the major events in each of the chapters in this section. Then complete the rest of the questions on this page.

2. How does Bilbo get separated from everyone?

   _____

   _____

3. In one well-written sentence, characterize Gollum.

   _____

   _____

4. After he does not guess the last riddle, why does Gollum go back to his island?

   _____

   _____

5. How do the Goblins and Wargs trap the party in the forest?

   _____

   _____

6. Why does the Lord of the Eagles save them?

   _____

   _____

7. Why must the dwarves enter Beorn's house in pairs, five minutes apart?

   _____

   _____

8. In one well-written sentence, characterize Beorn.

   _____

   _____

9. Why can't the party go around Mirkwood?

   _____

   _____

10. On the back of this page, predict what you think will happen to Bilbo and the dwarves in Mirkwood.

Magic

Magic plays a significant part in The Hobbit. It gets Bilbo and the dwarves out of several tight spots.

Sometimes, lack of knowledge makes things seem magical. When understood, most magic tricks are no longer magical. Can you think of something you know about that may have appeared magical in Bilbo's time? Do you think they would have thought a camera or a television set magical? Could you explain these mysterious things to Bilbo and his friends?

Here is a magic trick you can use to amaze your friends.

Magic Card!

Show a friend a greeting card made from a single folded piece of paper. Tell him or her that you are going to cut a hole in it and climb through.

1. Cut out a small strip from the center of the card along the fold, leaving about ½ inch at both ends.

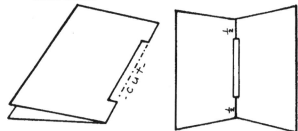

2. With card still folded, cut lines through both halves about ½ inch apart. Stop your cuts about ½ inch from the edge.

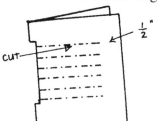

3. Turn card, and cut between each cut already made, stopping ½ inch before the folded edge.

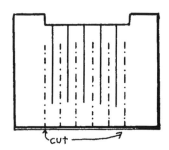

4. Carefully open card and stretch it out, pulling gently. You'll have a hole you can step through!

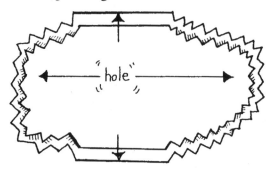

If magic interests you, check out a book of magic from your school or local library. Practice the tricks and put on a magic show! Perhaps your class can stage a magic show for another class or school assembly!

For another "magic trick," see page 47 in the answer key.

Can You Guess?

Gollum and Bilbo have a riddle contest deep in the underground tunnels of Misty Mountain. Their riddles use clues and hints to try to describe a specific thing—a mountain, teeth, daisies, dark, eggs, fish, and time.

With a partner, choose a common subject and brainstorm as many qualities as you can about it. Then, devise a four-lined to eight-lined riddle using the traits of the item. Try to make your riddle rhyme.

When each group has finished creating riddles, exchange them. Can you stump each other? Do you think your riddles would have stumped Bilbo or Gollum?

Subject: _____

List of qualities about the subject:

_____   _____   _____

_____   _____   _____

_____   _____   _____

_____   _____   _____

Write your finished riddle in the box below. Cut it out for the class riddle exchange!

Science: Weather Watch

Bilbo and the dwarves run into a terrible thunder and lightning storm. Described as more than a storm, it is a thunder-battle.

For many, many years, people throughout history were unaware of what caused storms and how weather happened. In today's world, weather is still sometimes unpredictable, but its causes are much more understood.

How much do you know about weather and its causes? Share what you know with the class and research to find out more about what you don't know. Here are some ideas to get you started.

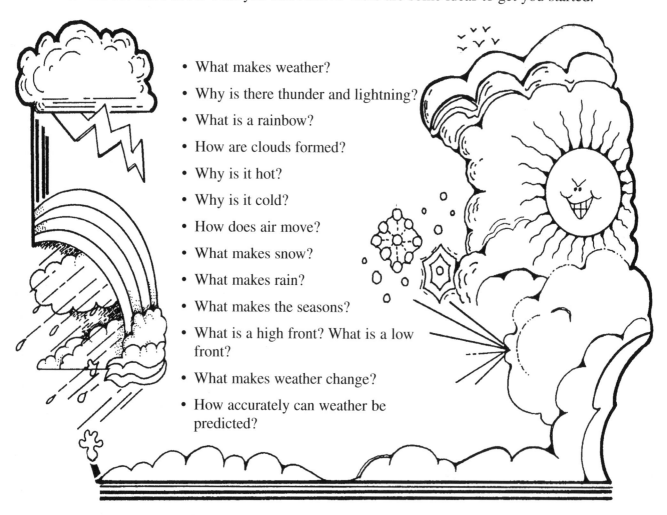

- What makes weather?
- Why is there thunder and lightning?
- What is a rainbow?
- How are clouds formed?
- Why is it hot?
- Why is it cold?
- How does air move?
- What makes snow?
- What makes rain?
- What makes the seasons?
- What is a high front? What is a low front?
- What makes weather change?
- How accurately can weather be predicted?

Here are some other ideas you may want to explore:

- Keep track of the weather for a month. Graph temperatures, precipitation, and other measurable data.
- Present a report or drama on lightning safety.
- Draw and label the types of clouds.
- Explain how Earth's motions affect its weather.
- Research weather-related careers.

"Out of the Frying Pan . . ."

The title of Chapter 6 is "Out of the Frying Pan into the Fire." This type of phrase is called a proverb. Proverbs are short, popular phrases or sentences containing truth. In Bilbo's situation, this phrase means he has gone from one danger into an even bigger one.

Below are some other common proverbs. Explain what you think each of them means.

"People who live in glass houses shouldn't throw stones."

"Stuck between a rock and a hard place."

"A cat in gloves catches no mice."

"No pain, no gain."

"A penny saved is a penny earned."

"That's the pot calling the kettle black."

"Let sleeping dogs lie."

"I'll cross that bridge when I come to it."

"Six of one, half a dozen of the other."

"Don't cry over spilt milk."

"In for a penny, in for a pound."

"Don't make a mountain out of a mole hill."

"You can't teach an old dog new tricks."

"Three may keep a secret if two of them are dead."

"One today is worth two tomorrows."

"If you can't stand the heat, get out of the kitchen."

"Better slip with foot than by tongue."

"A bird in the hand is worth two in the bush."

List other proverbs which are favorites of yours.

_____

_____

_____

_____

Which of these proverbs have been true in your life? Choose one from the list or that you have written and write an autobiographical incident in which you use the proverb as the theme of your writing. If you are willing, share your paper with others in your class.

Quiz

1. On the back of this paper, write a one paragraph summary of the major events in each of the chapters of this section. Then, complete the rest of the questions on this page.

2. What are the nights like in Mirkwood? Why can't they light fires?

   _____

3. Describe what happens to Bombur in Mirkwood.

   _____

   _____

4. Explain how Bilbo saves the dwarves from the giant spider.

   _____

   _____

   _____

5. Why do the Wood-elves capture and imprison the dwarves?

   _____

   _____

6. Explain how Bilbo helps the dwarves escape from the Wood-elves.

   _____

   _____

7. In one well-written sentence, characterize Thorin.

   _____

   _____

8. Describe the area around the mountain near the secret door.

   _____

   _____

9. How do Bilbo and the dwarves finally find the secret door?

   _____

   _____

10. Bilbo's personality has become quite different since the beginning of the story. On the back of this paper, describe these changes.

Disappearing Forests

Bilbo and the dwarves spend many days in Mirkwood, a deep, dark, and mysterious forest. Many animals and the Wood-elves are dependent on this forest for survival.

In today's world, forests are becoming endangered. The wood is cut for building needs, and the forest land is cleared to provide space for cities, farming, and ranching. Many people have never seen a real forest.

For this activity, you will work in small groups of two to four people. Each group will research, prepare, and present a lesson on forests to the class. Here are some ideas from which to choose.

- Discover what kinds of forests there are (redwood, tropical rain, everglade, etc.) and discuss the similarities and differences of each. Include answers to questions such as these:
    - What kinds of animals live in the forest?
    - What specifically is causing or might cause this forest to be endangered?
- Draw or make a relief map of the world. Color in the areas of rain forests.
- Make drawings of the trees found in different types of forests. Explain the use of each of the trees.
- Some scientists believe that the destruction of tropical rain forests is causing a "Greenhouse Effect." Explain this term.
- Research different ways forests could be conserved.
- Choose one specific kind of forest and explain in detail what varieties of animal life depend on this forest for survival.
- There are many National Parks, National Forests, and Wildlife Refuges protected by the government. Direct a letter to one of these protected environments, requesting information about its history and future. Share the information you receive.
- Many people argue that they have a right to the wood, natural resources, jobs, and food the forests provide. They do not believe in saving these forests for an unpredictable future. Research and discuss the pros and cons of this belief.
- How is the weather dependent on forests? Use graphs and charts in your explanation.

Describe the job of a forest or park ranger. What are his or her responsibilities? How hard is it to become a ranger? What schooling do you need? Invite a forest ranger to talk to your class as part of your report.

- Visit the nearest forest to your house. Take pictures and collect any brochures or information packets that are available. Look for forest life. Write a detailed report about what you saw.
- Research the types of animals that are endangered due to the destruction of their forest habitats.
- How does a forest grow, and how can it be destroyed?

Prejudices

Thorin Oakenshield and the dwarves are captured by the Wood-elves of Mirkwood, and thrown into the dungeons of the Elven king. The elves have no love of dwarves because in the early days of Middle Earth, they warred over treasure. Both elves and dwarves have accused each other of wrongdoings since their ancient wars. Because they are old enemies, neither will trust the other.

Often in life, groups of people carry on old hatreds of other groups. They prejudge how they believe these other people will be. This type of feud is often carried on through generation after generation.

In groups of two to four, create a story that dramatizes an example of prejudging. Within your story, show how this type of judgment can be overcome. Here are some ideas to help you get started.

- Brainstorm a list of group stereotypes. Write down how people expect these groups to behave.

- List conflicts that two of these groups might face if they were to meet each other.

- Write this conflict into a script. Assign parts and act out how these two groups might first act with each other.

- Brainstorm possible solutions to overcoming "first-impression" stereotypes. Add one or more of these ideas to your script.

- Determine if these two different groups could become friendly.

- Rehearse with this new scene, showing how it is possible to overcome prejudice.

- Put it all together and perform your drama for the class.

Your class may want to choose some of the better dramas to perform for other classes, a school assembly, or a parent night.

Social Studies: Mapmaking

Before we even begin reading The Hobbit, Tolkien's maps at the beginning of the book help us visualize the world we are about to discover. His character Bilbo utilizes maps as well. After studying Thorin's map, Bilbo convinces the dwarves to search the western slopes for the secret door.

Learning how to read and make maps is a valuable skill. If we can read maps, we know how to locate specific places and gather needed information. If we know how to make maps, we can increase our ability to communicate with others. Maps are fun to read and make, too!

Make a map of your school, your neighborhood, your backyard, your route home from school, your city, a favorite spot, or a fantasy place. Include a key that shows distance and identifies any specific symbols. When you are finished, show your map to a classmate and see if he or she can read it!

Here are some map symbols you may wish to cut out and attach to your own map.

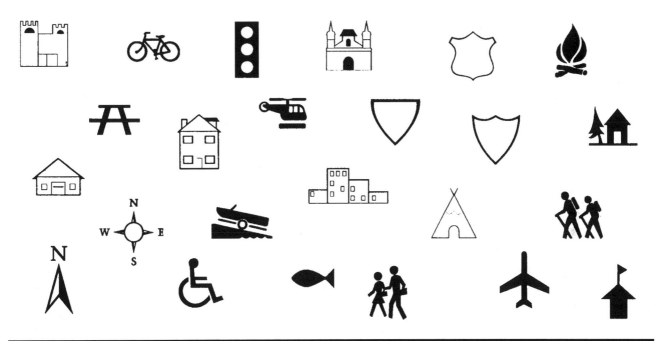

Map Key

Changes

When Gandalf first visits Bilbo, looking for someone to share in an adventure, Bilbo tells Gandalf that hobbits are:

". . . plain quiet folk and have no use for adventures. Nasty disturbing uncomfortable things! Make you late for dinner! I can't think what anybody sees in them. "

The dwarves are not quite sure that Bilbo will be able to handle the adventures at all, and Bilbo himself wonders how he found himself at The Green Dragon Inn, riding a pony away from Hobbiton.

However, Bilbo changes with each new challenge he meets, until he becomes the unspoken leader of the party. Without Bilbo, the dwarves would never have made it to Lonely Mountain.

Is an adventure something that happens to us or how we react to what happens? Often in life, adventures are not as obvious as killing giant spiders or escaping from an Elven king's dungeon. Sometimes adventures are made out of ordinary days and ordinary events, with ordinary people who become the heroes. You may not even realize you've been in an adventure until after it's over!

Think about times you have learned a new skill, moved, changed schools, competed in sports, welcomed a new pet, discovered a new friend, performed in front of an audience, or had a terrifying fall. These events are adventures in process. Have you grown or changed from your experience with any of these situations, as Bilbo grew and changed because of his adventure with the dwarves?

Recall a time when something happened to cause you to grow and change in a positive way. Then answer the questions below on a separate piece of paper. Use detail in all your answers.

1. What happened? Describe the event.

2. How did you react in the situation?

3. How did you feel when this happened?

4. Who else was affected by your actions?

5. How did this event change you?

6. What advice would you give someone who might experience the same type of "adventure"?

Quiz

1. On the back of this paper, write a one paragraph summary of the major events in each of the chapters in this section. Then, complete the questions on the rest of this page.

2. What does Smaug do when he discovers Bilbo has stolen the cup?

    _____

    _____

3. What do you determine to be the weak point of the dwarves' plan?

    _____

    _____

4. How does Bilbo describe himself when Smaug asks who he is and where he comes from?

    _____

    _____

5. In one well-written sentence, characterize Smaug.

    _____

    _____

6. What is cram?

    _____

    _____

7. What does Thorin give Bilbo?

    _____

    Why? _____

8. In one well-written sentence, characterize Bard.

    _____

    _____

9. What is the importance of the black arrow?

    _____

    _____

10. On the back of this paper, describe the Arkenstone of Thrain. Why does Bilbo keep it? Does he have a right to it?

Armor!

Tolkien makes references to armor several times in *The Hobbit*. He describes the importance of armor for the dwarves and has Thorin present Bilbo with a coat of armor that is fit for an Elf prince. Even Smaug is described as having "armour like ten-fold shields."

Originally, armor was confining and heavy, used only as protection against spears and swords. However, if armor were made today, it would probably be lightweight and formfitting, just like Bilbo's coat of armor.

Here are some armor-related activities for you to try.

- Research the use of armor throughout history. Draw or make models of the different types, including samples from the Greeks, Romans, Germans of the Middle Ages, the Europeans of the 1600's, and the French of the 1800's.

- During the Middle Ages, armor was used to protect horses as well as men. Draw and label examples of horse armor.

- Research the change from the type of armor used to protect from swords to the armor that had to protect from bullets.

- Design your own coat of armor using tinfoil, cardboard, and other material that is lightweight and pliable enough to fit around your body. Make sure it covers your arms and/or legs, yet leaves room for them to move freely. You may also want to design a helmet that is similar to your coat. Give your coat of armor a distinctive pattern that would signal you as a friend (or foe!) in the battlefield.

Here are several designs that were common in the days of Rome.

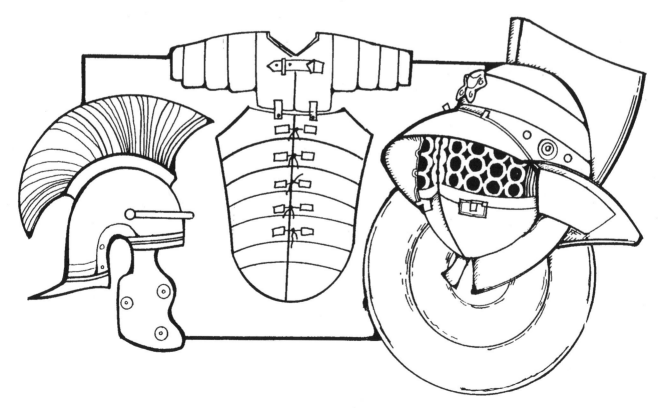

Talk Show!

Often, famous people are interviewed on television talk shows to give the general public a chance to find out more about them. The talk show host plans thoughtful, probing, and sometimes humorous questions to ask that will reveal information about the guest that is not common knowledge.

Working in groups of two to four, create a ten to fifteen minute talk show with your guests drawn from the characters in *The Hobbit*. Decide who will be the host and who will be the guests to be interviewed. Plan questions and answers for each character. Decide the order of your program. Provide and prepare for audience response.

When you have finished your preparation, present your "talk show" to the class.

Here are some possible "guests" for your show.

Thorin Oakenshield	Beorn	Master of the Town
one of the Spiders	a Warg	the Elven king
Great Goblin	Smaug	Bilbo Baggins
a Sackville-Baggins	Gollum	William the Troll
the Lord of the Eagles	Gandalf	Bard the Bowman

Language Arts: Further Adventures

Little did Bilbo guess when he left his comfortable home how many adventures he would soon have. His adventures fill *The Hobbit* and make for entertaining reading.

Create another adventure for Bilbo that might have been included in *The Hobbit*. Your adventure may happen within the forest of Mirkwood, the caves of Lonely Mountain, or any other appropriate setting. Bilbo can be alone in the adventure or accompanied by the dwarves, Gandalf, Gollum, Beorn, Smaug, or any other character you choose or invent. Your story should include a situation from which Bilbo must escape using some extraordinary means, such as Bilbo's ring, Gandalf's magic, a rescue by Eagles, a clever ruse, or any other imaginative solutions.

Write your story alone, with partners, or in a small group. If you are working with others, here is a technique you might like to try.

Story Pass

- Person #1 writes the first paragraph of the story and passes it to person #2.

- Person #2 clarifies any questions about what Person 1 intended, makes necessary corrections, and writes the second paragraph of the story. Person #2 then passes the story to Person #3.

- Person #3 clarifies any questions he or she might have about the previous writing, and makes the necessary changes. Then, Person #3 writes the third paragraph.

- This process continues, with group members rotating the story paper until the story is finished.

- The finished story is shared with the class.

Family Tree

In *The Hobbit,* family backgrounds are stressed, especially with introductions. Fathers, grandfathers, uncles, and grandmothers are often included when Tolkien describes a character.

Research your own family tree. Use the tree below to showcase your history.

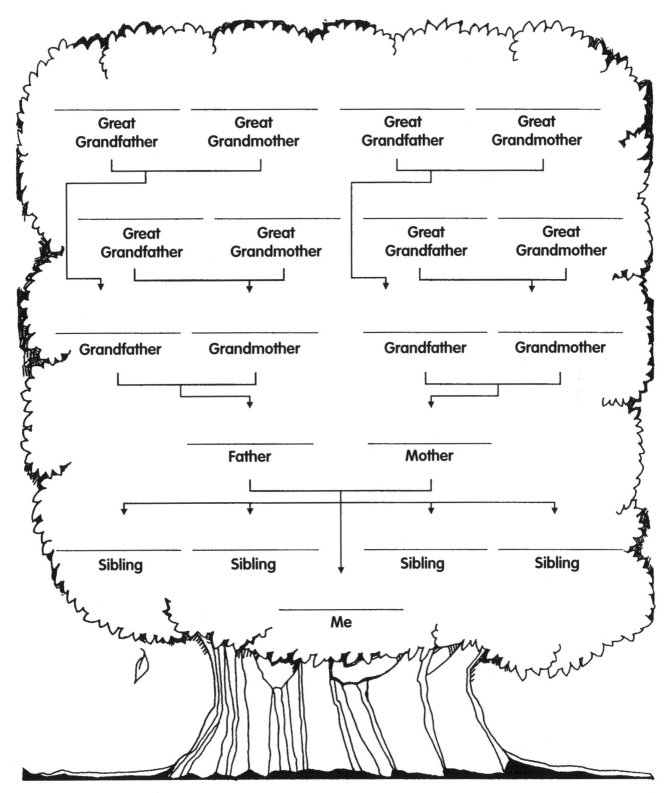

Quiz

1. On the back of this page, write a one paragraph summary of the main events in each of the chapters in this section. Then, complete the rest of the questions on this page.

2. What good news does Roac bring? What bad news does he bring?

   _____

   _____

3. Why does Thorin refuse Bard his requests for treasure?

   _____

   _____

4. Why does Bilbo offer the Arkenstone to Bard?

   _____

   _____

5. How has the treasure changed Thorin?

   _____

   _____

6. Who is involved in the Battle of Five Armies?

   _____

   _____

7. Why isn't Bilbo found until the day after the battle?

   _____

   _____

8. How does Thorin make amends with Bilbo?

   _____

   _____

9. Why are Bilbo's things being sold? What is it the Sackville-Bagginses never admit?

   _____

   _____

10. Throughout the book, the narrator interjects numerous comments, some humorous, some philosophical. On the back of this paper, give an example of one of these comments, and tell how you think it added (or detracted) from the story.

Fly Away!

Birds play an important part in *The Hobbit*, often saving lives or sharing valuable information.

How much do you know about birds? Working by yourself, with partners, or as a class, complete some or all of the bird-related projects described below.

- Draw a picture of the American bald eagle. Research where it lives, what it eats, and when and why it was chosen by the Congress to be the national emblem of the United States.

- Read "The Raven" by Edgar Allan Poe. Compare Poe's raven to Roac. Draw a picture of a raven. Research a raven's habits and habitats. Find information about crows and compare them to ravens.

- An old thrush gives Bilbo the information he needs to find the secret door. Draw a picture of a thrush. Research a thrush's habits and habitats.

- In *The Hobbit*, the eagles, ravens, and thrushes talk to mankind. Visit a pet store and find out what kinds of birds can be trained to talk. Tape record any talking birds in the store. Are there limitations to what a bird can be trained to say? How long does it take to train a bird to talk? What do you think would be the most interesting thing about owning a talking bird?

- Many people own birds as pets. Research and describe what is required to take care of a bird. Find out what types of birds make the best pets. If possible, bring a bird to class.

- Bird watching can be a rewarding pastime. Attracting birds to your home with food provides an easy way to watch them. Described below are directions for making two simple types of bird feeders. Keep a record of the types of birds that come to your feeders.

Pine Cone Bird Feeder

Wind a piece of wire around the top of a large pine cone so the wire is able to securely suspend the cone. Spread peanut butter over the entire surface of the cone using a spatula or knife. Then, roll the cone in bird seed or sunflower seeds. Attach the wire to a branch or other area good for bird-watching.

Grapefruit Bird Feeder

Hollow out half a grapefruit, leaving the rind. Punch three holes just below the rim of the halved grapefruit with a nail. Thread about twelve inches of strong string through each hole, and gather the loose, six inch ends together just above the rim. Tie these ends together securely and attach to another length of string. Fill it with water or bird seed and suspend it from a good bird-watching spot.

Middle Earth Gazette

Imagine you lived in the world of Middle Earth and worked for a newspaper. What types of things would you find newsworthy?

Working in groups of two to four, create a newspaper for the rest of your classmates to read and enjoy. Look through a local paper and see how it is laid out and what kinds of materials have been published. Your teacher will provide you with butcher paper for your layout. Remember, you may be as creative as you want, adding to the Middle Earth Gazette events that did not really happen in *The Hobbit,* but might have! Don't forget to include some pictures or illustrations. Here are some ideas to help you get started.

BANNER: Middle Earth Gazette or other "catchy" name

HEADLINES: Make sure each article has a headline that will draw readers to it.

FRONT PAGE: Include news articles that are most provocative, such as:

> "Bilbo Baggins Disappears"
>
> "Trolls Found Frozen"
>
> "Mysterious Happenings Invade Mirkwood"
>
> "Dragon Destroys Town"

MIDDLE PAGES: Include articles that stress the personal side of events, such as:

Feature Articles: "Gollum's Side of the Story"

> "Beorn: His Life and Loves"
>
> "My House Was Smashed by Smaug."

Sports Articles: "The Great Goblin Games"

> "Eagle Soaring"
>
> "Spider Spinning Contests"
>
> "Warg Hunting"

Editorials: *(opinions)* "Bilbo Should Have Stayed Home"

> "Creatures, Large and Small, Should Have the Right to Protect Their Homes"

BACK PAGES: Include a variety of items, such as:

Classified Ads: "Lost and Found"

> "For Sale"
>
> "Pets Need Homes"
>
> "Jobs"

Music Reviews: "Gollum and the Goblins"

> "Smaug and the Smaugettes"

Advice Columns: "Dear Gandalf, . . ."

> "Dear Elven king, . . ."

Food and Restaurants: "New Restaurant Opens in Mirkwood"

> "Anti-Venom Recipes"

ADVERTISEMENTS: Include ads that help to pay for the printing of the paper. Include artwork.

When you have finished your paper, share it with your class. You may want to read or summarize your best articles. Attach all finished papers to a class bulletin board for display.

Music: Middle Earth Songs

Throughout The Hobbit, songs play an important part in the description of the character and values of the dwarves, elves, goblins, and dragons.

This part of the dwarves' song in Chapter 1 sets the tone for adventure.

"Far over the misty mountains cold

To dungeons deep and caverns old

We must away, ere break of day,

To claim our long-forgotten gold."

This part of the goblins' song in Chapter 6 shows the reader their joy in killing.

"Bake and toast 'em, fry and roast 'em!

till beards blaze, and eyes glaze;

till hair smells and skins crack,

fat melts, and bones black

 in cinders lie

 beneath the sky!

 So dwarves shall die,

and light the night for our delight,

 Ya hey!

 Ya-harri-hey!

 Ya hoy!"

Even Bilbo joins in the creation of song as he sings to let the dwarves know he is near when they are trapped by the Spiders.

"Here am I, naughty little fly;

you are fat and lazy.

You cannot trap me, though you try,

in your cobwebs crazy."

Look through the book and re-read the songs found in Chapters 1, 3, 4, 6, 7, 8, 9, 10, 15, and 19. Notice the story each song tells.

Listen to recordings of Tolkien's songs of Middle Earth from one or more of the selections listed in the Bibliography (page 45). Or, you and your classmates might enjoy setting one of Tolkien's song lyrics to your own melody! Perhaps you might even want to try creating your own lyrics and melody for a song about Middle Earth!

Wise Advice

Roac, son of Carc, is 153 years old and has very sensible, wise advice for Thorin. Sometimes, those who are older have learned much through the experiences of their lives.

Do you get the chance to talk with your grandparents or someone else who has lived a long time? What do you like to talk about with them? What do they like to talk about with you?

Interview your grandparents or people from their generation. Use these ideas to help you get started in your interviews. Be sure to add your own ideas to the list as well.

SUGGESTED INTERVIEW TOPICS

Childhood: Tell me about:
- ◆ what the world was like.
- ◆ your time with your family.
- ◆ grade school experiences.
- ◆ hobbies and special interests.
- ◆ your heroes.
- ◆ a typical day.
- ◆ where you lived.
- ◆ your favorite music.
- ◆ what you did for fun.
- ◆ your pets.
- ◆ your favorite teacher.
- ◆ your responsibilities.
- ◆ special friends.
- ◆ your dreams.

The Teen Years: Tell me about:
- ◆ your first date.
- ◆ your most embarrassing moment.
- ◆ special friends.
- ◆ what the world was like.
- ◆ a typical day.
- ◆ hobbies and special interests.
- ◆ your first job.
- ◆ what you did for fun.
- ◆ your responsibilities.
- ◆ your first drive.
- ◆ your fears.
- ◆ your dreams.

Adulthood: Tell me about:
- ◆ your jobs.
- ◆ your marriage.
- ◆ your children.
- ◆ your grandchildren.
- ◆ what the world has been like.
- ◆ special friends.
- ◆ hobbies and special interests.
- ◆ food likes and dislikes.
- ◆ your responsibilities.
- ◆ your view of the world.
- ◆ a favorite poem or story.
- ◆ a great joy.
- ◆ a great sorrow.
- ◆ what you do best.
- ◆ military service.
- ◆ your dreams.
- ◆ advice you have for living the best life a person can.

Any Questions?

When you finished reading *The Hobbit*, did you have some questions that were left unanswered? Write some of your questions here.

_____

_____

_____

Work in groups or by yourself to prepare possible answers for some or all of the questions you have asked above and those written below. When you have finished your predictions, share your ideas with the class.

- Will Bilbo continue his adventuring ways?

- What happens to Gollum?

- Does Gollum ever try to get the ring back?

- Does Bilbo tell anyone at home about the ring and its power to make him invisible?

- Could the ring have other powers that we do not know about?

- How do you think Bilbo's neighbors would act if elves or other "unusual" creatures from Middle Earth came to visit him in Hobbiton?

- Do the Sackville-Bagginses influence any of the other hobbits in Hobbiton to doubt Bilbo Baggins's existence?

- Who is the Necromancer?

- Do the dwarves and elves ever get over their feud?

- Do you think if he hadn't died Thorin would have forgiven Bilbo? If Elrond had not read the moon runes, would the dwarves still have been able to get into the tunnel?

- Will goblins take over the Misty Mountains again?

- Could the Battle of Five Armies have been won without Beorn?

- Why did Gandalf say that Bilbo is only "quite a little fellow in a wide world after all"?

- What other kinds of magical creatures, good or bad, may have existed in Middle Earth?

- Which of the characters in The Hobbit do you think will be important in The Lord of the Rings?

Book Report Ideas

There are numerous ways to report on a book once you have read it.

After you have finished reading *The Hobbit,* choose one method of reporting on the book that interests you. It may be a way that your teacher suggests, an idea of your own, or one of the ways that is mentioned below.

- **See What I Read?**

  This report is a visual one. A model of a scene from the story can be created, or a likeness of one or more of the characters from the story can be drawn or sculpted.

- **Time Capsule**

  This report provides people living at a "future" time with the reasons *The Hobbit* is such an outstanding book, and gives these "future" people reasons why it should be read. Make a time capsule-type of design, and neatly print or write your reasons inside the capsule. You may wish to "bury" your capsule after you have shared it with your classmates. Perhaps one day someone will find it and read *The Hobbit* because of what you wrote!

- **Come To Life!**

  This report is one that lends itself to a group project. A size-appropriate group prepares a scene from the story for dramatization, acts it out, and relates the significance of the scene to the entire book. Costumes and props will add to the dramatization!

- **Into the Future**

  This report predicts what might happen if *The Hobbit* were to continue with Bilbo Baggins as the hero. It may take the form of a story in narrative or dramatic form, or a visual display.

- **A Letter**

  In this report, write to the publishers of *The Hobbit.* Tell them what you liked about the story and ask them for answers to questions you may have about the writing of the book. After your teacher has read it, and you have made your writing the best it can be, send it to the publishing company.

- **Guess Who or What!**

  This report takes the form of several games of "Twenty Questions." The reporter gives a series of clues about a character from the story in a vague to precise, general to specific order. After all clues have been given, the identity of the mystery character must be deduced. After the character has been guessed, the same reporter presents another "Twenty Questions" about an event in the story.

- **A Character Comes To Life!**

  Suppose one of the characters in The Hobbit came to life and walked into your home or classroom? This report gives a view of what this character sees, hears, and feels as he or she experiences the world in which you live.

- **Sales Talk**

  This report serves as an advertisement to "sell" *The Hobbit* to one or more specific groups. You decide on the group to target and the sales pitch you will use. Include some kind of graphics in your presentation.

- **Coming Attraction!**

  The Hobbit is about to be re-made into a movie and you have been chosen to design the promotional poster. Include the title and author of the book, a listing of the main characters and the contemporary actors who will play them (or their voices), a drawing of a scene from the book, and a paragraph synopsis of the story.

- **Literary Interview**

  This report is done in pairs. One student will pretend to be a character in the story, steeped completely in the persona of his or her character. The other student will play the role of a television or radio interviewer, trying to provide the audience with insights into the character's personality and life. It is the responsibility of the partners to create meaningful questions and appropriate responses.

- **The Perfect Gift**

  For this report, you will be responsible for choosing a different and appropriate gift for three of the characters from The Hobbit. Your gifts must be selected from the items you have available to you. Describe or draw a picture of each gift, name the person it will be given to, and explain why it is the perfect gift for him or her.

- **Standard Form**

  This report is a standard report in which story elements are defined and supported with examples from The Hobbit. Areas to include are a plot summary, character analysis, setting description, theme explanation, and a personal evaluation of the story.

Research Ideas

Describe three things you read in The Hobbit that you would like to learn more about.

1. _____

2. _____

3. _____

As you are reading *The Hobbit*, you will encounter fantasy characters and lands that were unknown before Tolkien's book was published in 1937. Today, fantasy literature is one of the most popular forms of story writing, and hundreds of elves, dwarves, halflings, wizards, goblins, dragons, and other magical creatures can be found abundantly in books!

Work in groups to research one or more of the areas you named above, or the areas that are mentioned below. Share your findings with the rest of the class in any appropriate form of oral presentation.

Background histories of:

◆ dwarves

◆ elves

◆ halflings

◆ dragons

◆ wizards

◆ sorcerers

◆ unicorns

Check your local library for a complete, up-to-date-listing of fantasy selections. Take notes below. Then plan to read at least one additional fantasy novel.

Other Famous Fantasy Novels

_____

_____

_____

_____

Other Fantasy Worlds

_____

_____

_____

_____

Other Famous Fantasy Characters

_____

_____

_____

Other Fantasy Heroes and Villains

_____

_____

_____

Travel Middle Earth!

Imagine what a vacation in Middle Earth would be like!

Create a contemporary travel brochure for the Land of Middle Earth. Your brochure should try to convince people that Middle Earth would be the best place to vacation! You may want to visit a local travel agency to collect examples of professional travel brochures to help you with your design. You must be exact and descriptive, for people want to know why they should spend their vacation money on Middle Earth, rather than some other advertised spot. See pages 39 and 40 for brochure directions and sample graphics.

Here are some things you might include in your brochure.

- An attractive, attention-getting cover with a catchy title

- A detailed map of Middle Earth, starring and identifying points of interest to travelers

- Detailed maps of specific regions of Middle Earth

- Reasons why Middle Earth should be visited

- Tips for the selection of the best travel guides

- Climate information

- Suggested items needed for the journey

- Information about transportation to and through Middle Earth

- Accommodation recommendations, such as the best hotels, motels, campsites, and caves

- Dining guide and sample menus (See page 41 for ideas.)

- Spots visitors to Middle Earth must not miss

- Recreational activities

- Inhabitants of Middle Earth "friendliness" guide

- Suggestions for short "day hikes" visitors can take

- Dangers that may be encountered while traveling through Middle Earth

- Shopping tips

- Discount coupons for food, attractions, and/or lodging

- "Words to Learn" list to help visitors communicate with Middle Earth residents

- Pictures of places, events, and creatures that will stimulate the desire to see Middle Earth

- Quotes from other visitors about how much they enjoyed their vacations in Middle Earth

- Anything else that will promote travel in Middle Earth

Travel Middle Earth!

Travel brochures are often folded in thirds, with something very appealing on the front and back. The other information is arranged neatly on the inside.

Directions:

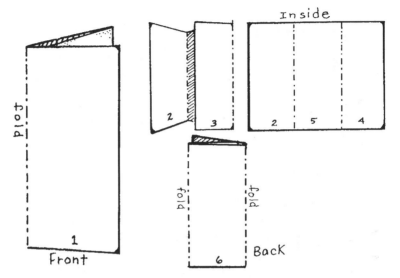

- Fold a sheet of paper in thirds as shown in the diagram. The paper needs to be at least 8½ inches by 11 inches. Be sure that your last fold is the left over right fold.

- Plan the information that will be presented on each fold of the brochure. You will have six areas to fill.

- Remember to have something on the front cover that will make your prospective vacationers want to pick up the brochure!

Travel Middle Earth!

Here are some symbols and graphics you may want to use as you design your Middle Earth Brochure!

Travel Middle Earth!

Here are some ideas for dining discounts for Middle Earth restaurants. You may want to fill in these coupons with a menu item on special at a specific dining place, or create restaurant and coupon ideas of your own.

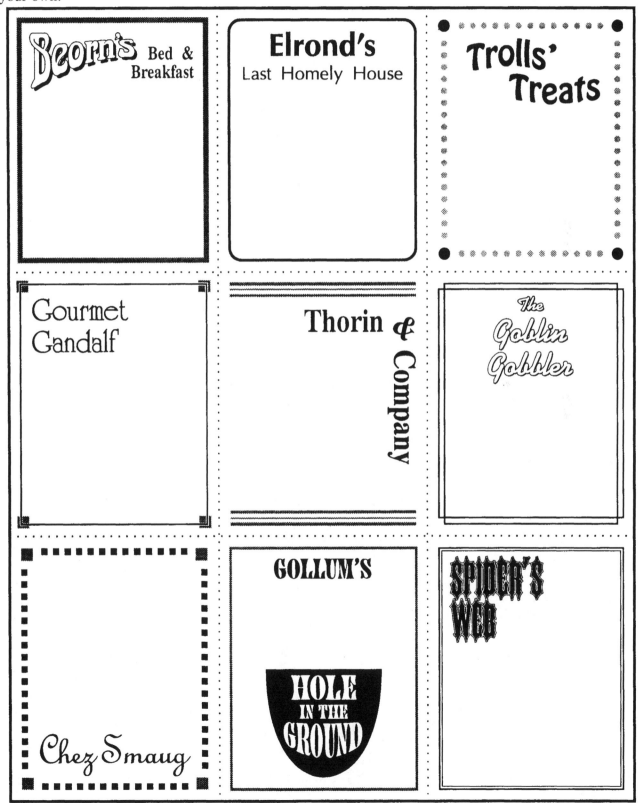

Unit Test

Matching

Match the names of the characters with their descriptions.

1. _____ Gandalf
2. _____ Thorin Oakenshield
3. _____ Beorn
4. _____ Elrond
5. _____ Bombur
6. _____ Smaug
7. _____ Roac
8. _____ Gollum
9. _____ Dain
10. _____ Bard

a. small, slimy, dark creature
b. skin changer
c. son of Nain
d. a gigantic, red-gold dragon
e. chief of the great ravens
f. dwarf who falls into the enchanted river in Mirkwood
g. Elf lord and rune reader
h. archer who kills the dragon
i. wandering wizard
j. dwarf leader of the expedition

True or False

Write true or false next to each statement below. On the back of this test paper, explain why each false answer is false.

1. _____ Bilbo leaves on the adventure with the dwarves because he lives a discontented life.
2. _____ The destination of the dwarves and Bilbo is the Lonely Mountain.
3. _____ The wild wolves that run with the goblins are called Wargs.
4. _____ The last battle fought in the book is called The Battle of Five Armies.
5. _____ All in Hobbiton rejoice when Bilbo returns from his adventure.

Short Answer

Provide a short answer for each of these questions.

1. The name of the forest through which Bilbo and the dwarves must travel is called

   _____

2. This was Gollum's "birthday present." _____

3. What happens to an elven sword when it comes near goblins? _____

   _____

4. Bilbo tells Smaug that they have not come just for treasure, but also for _____

5. Bilbo names his memoirs _____

Essay

1. In the last chapter, the narrator reveals that Bilbo has lost his reputation. Explain why on the back of this paper.

2. Originally, Bilbo is chosen to be the lucky number. Discuss how much of Bilbo's success on the adventure is due to luck, how much to skill, and how much to cunning.

Response

Explain the meaning of each of these quotations from *The Hobbit*.

Chapter 1   " 'We are plain quiet folk and have no use for adventures. Nasty disturbing uncomfortable things! Make you late for dinner! I can't think what anybody sees in them.' "

Chapter 5   " 'What's a burrahobbit got to do with my pocket, anyways?'

Bilbo pinched himself and slapped himself; he gripped on his little sword; he even felt in his pocket with his other hand. There he found the ring he had picked up in the passage and forgotten about.

'What have I got in my pocket?' he asked aloud."

Chapter 5   " 'Where is it? Where iss it?' Bilbo heard him crying. 'Losst it is, my precious, lost, lost! Curse us and crush us, my precious is lost!' "

Chapter 6   "Tonight the Lord of the Eagles was filled with curiousity to know what was afoot; so he summoned many other eagles to him, and they flew away from the mountains, and slowly circling ever round and round they came down, down, down towards the ring of the wolves and the meeting-place of the goblins."

Chapter 7   " 'A very good tale!' said he. 'The best I have heard for a long while. If all beggars could tell such a good one, they might find me kinder. You may be making it all up, of course, but you deserve supper for the story all the same. Let's have something to eat.' "

Chapter 8   " 'I will give you a name,' he said to it, 'and I shall call you Sting!' "

Chapter 12   " 'You have nice manners for a thief and a liar,' said the dragon. 'You seem familiar with my name, but I don't seem to remember smelling you before. Who are you and where do you come from, may I ask?' "

Chapter 12   " 'Never laugh at live dragons, Bilbo you fool!' he said to himself, and it became a favourite saying of his later, and passed into a proverb."

Chapter 14   " 'Arrow!' said the bowman. 'Black arrow! I have saved you to the last. You have never failed me and always I have recovered you. I had you from my father and he from of old. If ever you came from the forges of the true king under the Mountain, go now and speed well!' "

Chapter 16   " 'This is the Arkenstone of Thrain,' said Bilbo, 'the Heart of the Mountain; and it is also the heart of Thorin. He values it above a river of gold. I give it to you. It will aid you in your bargaining.' "

Chapter 17   " 'The Eagles! The Eagles!' he shouted. 'The Eagles are coming.' Bilbo's eyes were seldom wrong. The eagles were coming down the wind, line after line, in such a host as must have gathered from all the eyries of the North."

Chapter 19   " 'You are a very fine person, Mr. Baggins, and I am very fond of you, but you are only quite a little fellow in a wide world after all!' "

Conversations

Work in size-appropriate groups to write and perform the conversations that might have occurred in each of the following situations.

- Two of Bilbo's neighbors show up at his door the morning after the dwarves have visited and want to know what has been going on. (3 people)

- William, Bert, and Tom (the trolls) are sitting around the fire before Bilbo comes, discussing their latest adventure. (3 people)

- Thorin and Balin try to convince the Great Goblin to let them go after being captured in Misty Mountains. (3 people)

- Two goblins discuss the mysterious disappearance of some of their friends in the lower tunnels. (2 people)

- Gollum explains to Bilbo how he got the ring as a "birthday present." (2 people)

- The King of Eagles talks with Beorn about the unrest in the forest. (2 people)

- Beorn has a housekeeper who tells the dwarves and Bilbo about some of Beorn's other guests. (3 or more people)

- The Elven king hires the spiders to protect his forest. (2 or 3 people)

- Bilbo overhears two elves talking about the ancient feud between dwarves and elves. (2 people)

- Thorin tells Bilbo his version of the ancient feud between the elves and the dwarves. (2 people)

- The elves, pushing the heavy barrels with poles, decide to open them up to determine why they are so heavy. (3 or more people)

- The Master of Laketown talks with Bard about his suspicions concerning Bilbo and the party of dwarves. (2 people)

- A mouse in Smaug's cave tells Bilbo some of Smaug's secrets. (2 people)

- Gandalf stops Bilbo before he goes back up to the mountain and tells him where he has been and what he has been doing during the time he was away from the party. (2 people)

- Dain, Thorin, Gandalf, the Elven king, and Bard get together and discuss strategies before the Battle of Five Armies. (5 people)

- Bilbo discusses "movie rights" to his story with a producer. (2 people)

- The Sackville-Bagginses discuss with Bilbo's neighbors why they don't think Bilbo is the real Bilbo Baggins. (4 people)

- Write and perform one of your own conversation ideas for the characters from *The Hobbit.*

Bibliography

Abrams, Kathleen and Lawrence. *Logging and Lumbering.* (Julian Messner, 1980)

Baker, James. *Birthday Magic.* (Lerner Publishers, 1988)

Carpenter, Humphrey. *Tolkien: A Biography.* (Houghton, 1977)

Clarkson, Evan. *Eagles.* (WaylandPress,1981)

Elden, Peter. *Trickster's Handbook.* (Sterling 1989)

Farb, Peter. *The Forest.* (Time-Life Books, 1980)

Foster, Robert. *A Guide to Middle Earth.* (Mirage Press, 1971)

Green, Carol. *I Can Be a Forest Ranger.* (Childrens Press, 1989)

Grotta, Daniel. *Biography of J.R.R. Tolkien, Architect of Middle-Earth.* (RunningPress,1978)

Heady, Eleanor. *Trees are Forever—How They Grow from Seeds to Forests.* (Parents Press, 1978)

Helms, Randel. *Tolkien's World.* (Houghton, 1974)

Herbert, Don, and Hy Ruchlis. *Mr. Wizard's 400 Experiments in Science.* (Book Lab, 1983)

Hess, Lilo. *Bird Companion.* (Charles Scribnerand Sons, 1981)

Kocher, Paul H. *Master of Middle-Earth: The Fiction of J.R.R. Tolkien.* (Houghton, 1972)

Lampton, Christopher. *Endangered Species.* (Franklin Watts, 1988)

Leeny, Joseph. *Real Book of Magic.* (Garden City Books, 1951)

McCoy, J. J. *Lords of the Sky.* (Bobs Merrill, 1963)

McGrath, Susan. *How Animals Talk.* (National Geographic Society, 1955)

Noel, Ruth S. *The Mythology of Middle Earth.* (Houghton, 1977)

Peattie, Charles. *Paper Maché.* (Wayland,1977)

Pierce, Georgia. *Junior Science Book of Birdlife.* (Barrard, 1962)

Prosser, Robert. *Disappearing Rain Forests.* (Dryad Press, 1991)

Robbins, Chandler, et al. *Birds of North America.* (Western Publishing 1983)

Rogers, Cyril. *Seed-Eating Birds as Pets.* (Charles Scribner and Sons, 1974)

Schendler, George. *Presto-Magic for the Beginner.* (Dorset, 1977)

Simkins, Michael. *Warriors of Rome.* (Blandford, 1988)

Steven, Bill. *Magic Shows You Can Give.* (David McKay, 1965)

Stoddard, Charles. *Essentials of Forestry Practice.* (John Wiley and Sons, 1978)

Stone, Lynn. *Rain Forest Ecology.* (Rourke Enterprises, 1989)

Sutts, Ann and Myron. *Wildlife of the Forests.* (Abrams, 1979)

Tolkien, J.R.R.

The Hobbit. (Ballantine,1988)
The Lord of the Rings. (Ballantine, 1965)
Farmer Giles of Ham [and] *The Adventures of Tom Bombadil.* (UnwinBooks,1975)
Smith of Wootton Major. (Houghton, 1967)
The Father Christmas Letters. (Houghton, 1979)
The Silmarillion. (Houghton, 1977)
Unfinished Tales of Numenor and Middle-Earth. (Houghton, 1980)
The Pictures of J.R.R. Tolkien. (Houghton, 1979)

Tyler, J.E.A. *The Tolkien Companion.* (St. Martin's, 1976)

Wilkes, John. *The Roman Army.* (Lerner,1977)

Answer Key

Page 10

1. Accept appropriate responses.

2. Tales and extraordinary adventures sprouted up wherever Gandalf went. He was a wandering wizard with a reputation for amazing magical feats, wonderful storytelling and particularly excellent fireworks.

3. The dwarves want to go over the Misty Mountains to "dungeons deep and caverns old"; they wish to win back a "gleaming, golden hoard"; they left because a fearsome dragon "laid low their towers and houses frail."

4. Bilbo's job is to be the Burglar, the one who steals back the dwarves' treasure. He is also to be the 14th party member to break the "bad luck' of the number of 13 dwarves.

5. The significance of the map is that it belonged to Thor, Thorin's grandfather. It is a plan of Lonely Mountain, and contains runes that mark a hidden passage into the lower halls, and the lost treasure of the dwarves.

6. Bilbo gets caught the first time as he tries to nab a purse from out of the pocket of William the Troll.

7. Gandalf uses his voice to pretend he is one of the trolls, and keeps them arguing amongst themselves until dawn when the sun comes up and turns them to stone.

8. Rune letters are mysterious letters, made of an "alphabet" needing to be translated by someone versed in "reading the language." Moon letters are rune letters that you cannot see unless the moon shines behind them. The more cunning the author, the more "tricky" the letters. For example, you may only see some moon letters if they are read with a moon the same shape and season in which the letters were written.

9. Elrond tells the party that their swords are not troll-made, but Elven-made. They are famous blades—Orcrist, the Goblin Cleaver and Glamdring the Foe Hammer.

Page 15

1. Accept appropriate responses.

2. Bilbo is riding on Dori's shoulders when he is grabbed from behind. He rolls off Dori's shoulders, bumps his head, and is lost in the blackness.

3. Accept appropriate responses.

4. Gollum goes back to his island to get the ring of invisibility. He plans to put it on and come back and eat Bilbo.

5. The goblins and Wargs surround the dwarves, Gandalf, and Bilbo, forcing them to climb into the tree tops.

6. Gandalf had once rendered a service to the eagles and healed their lord from an arrow wound.

7. Beorn does not like company. Gandalf is going to spread out how often the dwarves arrive to correspond with his story about their adventures. The story distracts Beorg from counting how many dwarves there actually are.

8. Accept appropriate responses.

9. They cannot go around Mirkwood because it is 200 miles out of the way to the north, and twice that to the south. There are also no safe trails in the wild.

Answer Key *(cont.)*

Page 16

Here is a page of "magic" to share with your students!

I Know Your Number!

Tell your friend that you can guess two numbers he or she is thinking of, if he or she will do a mathematics problem with you.

Ask this friend to choose a number between 1 and 99 and a number between 5 and 50. Do not ask him or her what the numbers are. Then, give a piece of paper and these directions to your friend.

1. Write down the second number and multiply it by 2.
2. Add 5 to the total from step #1.
3. Multiply the total from step #2 by 100.
4. Divide the #3 total by 2.
5. Subtract the days in a year (365) from the #4 total.
6. Ask your friend to add the "secret first number" to the #5 total, without telling you what the number is.
7. Ask for the total to #6.
8. Secretly add 115 to the total your friend has given you..

The two digits on the right of your answer will be the first number your friend chose. The two digits on the left will be the second number chosen. Here is an example.

SECRET NUMBER #1 - 59

SECRET NUMBER #2 - 33

1. 2x33=66
2. 66+5=71
3. 71 x 100 = 7100
4. 7100 divided by 2 = 3550
5. 3550 - 365 = 3185
6. 3185 +59 = 3244
7. 3244

8. 3244 + 115 = 3359

right two digits 59

left two digits 33

Page 20

1. Accept appropriate responses.
2. The nights in Mirkwood are pitch black with gleaming eyes. Lighting fires brought huge, hand-sized moths by the hundreds.
3. Bombur tumbles into an enchanted stream and falls deeply asleep because of the magical waters.
4. Bilbo saves the dwarves by putting on his ring and, while invisible, leads the spiders away from the dwarves. He kills many of them with his sword, Sting.
5. They capture the dwarves because they have a mistrust of all strangers, especially dwarves. The dwarves had trespassed in their forest.
6. Bilbo steals the keys from the chief Elf-guard, who has fallen asleep because of the effect of some strong wine. Bilbo then unlocks the cells of the dwarves and takes them to the water gate. Here he puts them in empty barrels, which are pushed unknowingly by elves tending the moving of freight. The barrels are carried downstream and out of the area the Wood-elves "control."
7. Accept appropriate responses.
8. The land around Lonely Mountain is desolate and empty, rocky and barren.
9. Bilbo has carefully studied the map, and finds the area of the door. On Durin's Day, as he is sitting and studying the closed mountain walls, a thrush knocks a snail against the wall, alerting Bilbo to the soon-to-come ray of light which will point to the crack of the secret passage. Bilbo calls Thorin for the key, which is then used to open the secret door.

Answer Key (cont.)

Page 25

1. Accept appropriate responses.
2. Smaug is furious when he discovers his cup has been stolen. He flies out of his cave in a rage, shooting fire at the mountain and eating the dwarves' ponies.
3. The weak point of their plan is how to get rid of Smaug.
4. Bilbo describes himself in terms of the adventures he has had, such as the clue-finder, the stinging fly, the Ringwinner, and Barrel-rider. Accept other accurate responses.
5. Accept appropriate answers.
6. Cram is a bisquit-ish food, able to be kept indefinitely, sustaining, and unappealing to eat.
7. Thorin gives Bilbo a small coat of mail made out of a special silver steel which the elves call mithril.
8. Accept appropriate answers.
9. The black arrow has never failed Bard, and he has always been able to recover it. It came from the forges of the true king under the mountain.

Page 30

1. Accept appropriate responses.
2. The good news is that Smaug is dead. The bad news is that the men of Laketown and the Wood-elves are coming to claim a portion of the treasure.
3. Thorin will not parley with armed men at his gate, nor will he talk about sharing his treasure with the elves who held him prisoner.
4. Bilbo offers the Arkenstone to Bard as a bargaining tool. He believes that Thorin will do anything to get the Arkenstone back, including bargaining with Bard.
5. Thorin has become blind to anything but the treasure, including reason.
6. The Battle of Five Armies involves the men, the elves, the dwarves on one side, and the Wargs and the goblins on the other side.
7. While wearing his ring, Bilbo is knocked unconscious. He is invisible.

8. Thorin calls Bilbo to his side before he dies, and apologizes. He tells Bilbo that he wishes more people valued food, cheer, and song above hoarded gold.
9. Bilbo's things are being sold because everyone in Hobbiton presumed Bilbo was dead. The Sackville-Bagginses never admit he is the true Bilbo Baggins.

Pages 38–41

Create a bulletin board display of these culminating activities.

Page 42

Matching:

1. i   3. b   5. f   7. e   9. c
2. j   4. g   6. d   8. a   10. h

True or False

1. False; Bilbo leads a contented life.
2. True
3. True
4. True
5. False; some, specifically the Sackville-Bagginses, are quite disappointed

Short Answer

1. Mirkwood
2. the invisible ring
3. It glows
4. revenge
5. There and Back Again

Essay

1. Accept appropriate responses.
2. Accept appropriate responses.

Page 43

Accept all reasonable and well-supported answers.

Page 44

Perform the conversations in class. Ask students to respond to the conversations in several different ways, such as, "Are the conversations realistic?" or, "Are the words the characters say in keeping with their personalities?"